How To Write Kill Your Startup

"Easy tips for the non-writer"

By Steve Ash

How To Write Killer Content For Your Startup by Steve Ash, published by CommsBreakdown www.commsbreakdown.com

© 2019 Steve Ash

Table of contents

Introduction: Why You Need Killer Content

You've had your business idea. You've got the funding. And you're ready to start trading, winning customers and getting your new startup brand out there into the world.

But how do you tell people just how amazing your new business is?

Everyone knows that content marketing is one way to promote your startup, but no-one knows exactly how to create the right content – to a non-writer, it can seem rather daunting!

- How do you get content ideas?
- How do you spin them out into a series of blogs?
- Where do you get the practical, technical guidance you need?
- How do you define your brand style and tone?
- And how do you get your writing skills up to scratch?

This book gives you easy content-creation tips for the non-writer – so your content does the best possible job of marketing your product, engaging with customers and raising brand awareness. If you're a founder, entrepreneur or startup owner, you'll get the tools, advice and knowledge needed to create effective content for your startup.

End-to-end content creation

We'll start with the basics of defining your core vision and brand personality – the foundations for your writing style. Then we'll move on to improving your writing, planning your content and tailoring your writing for the main online, digital and social media channels you'll be using.

You can read this book in one sitting if you want (you might need a few coffees along the way, though!). Or you can dip into each chapter as your startup journey evolves and you need more specific advice on customising your content.

We'll be keeping the chapters short and easy to read, but with as much practical advice as possible crammed in there. Even if the longest thing you've ever written is a shopping list, you'll soon be writing engaging and exciting blogs, marketing copy, news stories, campaign content and social media posts.

So, let's start crafting the killer content that will drive your startup success…

1: Define Your Vision –
Missions and manifestos

Before you write a single word of content, you need to have an incredibly clear idea of WHY you're in business – and, by logical progression, why you're writing content to promote the central business idea behind your startup.

That core vision drives the business forward, and gives focus, purpose and relevance to the content you create – so let's make sure you get these foundations right!

Define WHY you're in business

Many startups are born from a personal passion. You find a hobby, an activity or an industry that you love, and you decide to turn that passion into a business. You come up with a unique business idea, or a new kind of widget/app/service, and you decide that now's the time to strike out on your own and start a business.

So, you know WHAT you do – your make widgets. But do you know WHY you're making them? What's the core driver behind your business existing in the first place?

This concept is something that the business writer Simon Sinek talks about in depth in his 'Start With Why' book – and I'd definitely suggest you dip into this book to get the full lowdown on the importance of defining this fundamental WHY.

In short, though, you and your fellow founders need to sit down and do some serious thinking about the nature of your business:

- What's your core vision for the firm?
- What are you aiming to bring to your customers?
- How do you differ from your competitors?
- Where are you truly adding value as a company?

By getting some detailed (and honest) answers to these questions, you can start to move towards defining your vision and outlining your mission as a business.

Outline your core values

What do values have to do with your content? Well, if your content is going to be an adequate representation of your brand, it needs to reflect what you believe in.

As we'll see in more depth in Chapter 3, Create Your Brand, your brand and your content should have real personality. And it's your values, your ethical standpoint and your beliefs as a founder that will define the initial personality behind your brand.

Sit down and ask yourself a few questions:

- **What do you believe in as a founder?** Are you driven by profit and an ambitious desire to meet targets? Or is your driver to make the world a better place by bringing your unique offering to the customers that need it?

- **What values do you want your startup to stick to?** Is it important to be human in your customer relationships? Or is having a good social impact something you want your people to think about?

- **How will your values drive your core mission?** Do you want to be an ethical business where having a positive impact is central to your mission? Or is providing the very best customer service your key goal for the business?

Write your manifesto

Your manifesto is the document that forms the beating heart of your startup.

Having a good business plan and a profitable business model are all vital elements of the financial side of your startup, but it's your manifesto that truly tells people who you are, what you're about – and gives your whole business journey some purpose.

Your manifesto must outline:

- **Your vision** – the reason WHY you're in business
- **Your aims** – what you want your startup to ACHIEVE as a business
- **Your core values** – the values that drive HOW you'll achieve your aims

Combining these core elements together into a formal document helps you bring your overriding mission together into a manifesto for the business – a document that explains the real DNA of your business and how it's going to interact with the world.

KEY TAKEAWAY: Have a core vision and know WHY you're in business

2: Know Your Audience – Customers and targets

You now know WHY you're in business, but do you understand the needs and expectations of your customers and prospects?

To write content that engages with your customers, you need to know WHO you're targeting, what their needs are and what their preferred communication channels will be. Without that information, you might as well just stand at the top of a mountain with a loud hailer, shouting information about your product features into the wind.

So, how do you improve your focus on the right customers?

Define your core audience

To start with, let's pin down who your core audience is. These are your ideal customers, and the people who (you hope) will come rushing to your website, ready to buy your product once it reaches the minimum viable product (MVP) stage and is ready to hit the market.

Knowing who you're targeting with your products/services is absolutely fundamental to the content you write, so it's important to define your audience and give yourself as concrete an idea as possible of your ideal customer.

Some key questions to ask yourself will include:

- **Are we selling to consumers or businesses?** – selling business-to-consumer (B2C) is a different kind of marketing to selling business-to-business (B2B). Knowing whether you have a consumer or business-focused product is vital to getting your content written, targeted and delivered to the correct audience.

- **What kind of consumer are you targeting?** – if you're going the B2C route, you need to pin down some key demographics around your ideal consumer. How old are they? What income bracket are they in? Where do they live? This will all help you later on when targeting your content and advertising to the right people.

- **Who's your key business audience?** – if you're a B2B business, you need to think slightly differently about your target audience. What type of business are you targeting? What industries are you focused on? Who are the key decision-makers and budget-holders in your target business?

Do some customer research

The more detailed you can be about the specifics of your core audience, the easier it will be to target your content effectively. So, investing time (and possibly money) in some drilled-down customer research is essential.

You need to get a good feel for who your ideal customers are, what their basic needs are and – most importantly – why they'd be interested in buying your product.

Talk to other businesses in your sector, do some desk research or get out and actually talk face-to-face with your prospects and potential customers. And, if finances allow, think about commissioning a professional market research company to build up a profile of your key customer audience or audiences.

Get to know what makes your customers tick and give your startup the best possible idea of your 'ideal customer persona'.

Flesh out those customer personas

Having defined your core audience and done your research, you need to formalise all this into a more concrete overview of your customer base.

Get granular with outlining the demographics of your ideal customers and put some flesh on the bones of your customer personas. The more tangible these personas are, the more refined you can be with your marketing and content creation.

Try to outline some core customer elements:

- **Outline your customer personas** – describe what your ideal customers are like as people and, based on your research and feedback, build up as broad a persona as possible for the people you're targeting.

- **Know the customer's needs** – have a very clear understanding of why a customer needs your product, what problem/pain it solves and what their expectations will be of your product, service or solution.

- **Define the best content channels to use** – research your core demographic and find out which marketing and social media channels they're most likely to use. By tailoring your content to the right channels, you focus your efforts in the right areas, and increase the chances of your content being read.

- **Understand where customers search for your products** – the majority of consumers and business buyers will make an initial product search online, but factor in whether bricks & mortar shops, or B2B outlets are part of your strategy.

KEY TAKEAWAY: Know who your customers are, and target them effectively

3: Create Your Brand – Personality, style and tone

You know the demographics and personality of your ideal customers, and you also know the core vision behind your own business model.

Now's the time to bring these two elements together into a brand that promotes your core vision, while attracting and engaging with your key target customers – the people who your content and marketing will be aimed at.

Create a personality for your brand

When we talk about a brand, we don't just mean your name, logo and colour palette. We're talking about an overriding brand that incorporates your vision, your values, your tone and (most importantly) the personality that comes across in the marketplace.

Personality is what makes your startup stand out in the crowded startup market. If your brand was a person, what kind of person would they be? Will your personality to be that of a professional expert, or are you aiming for a more human, chatty persona?

The nature of this brand personality will come from a mixture of sources, including:

- **Your personality as a founder** – in the early days, you ARE the business, so your own persona is going to be the real driver behind your startup brand. If you're reserved and professional, that will come across in your customer interactions. If you're energetic and lively, your brand will also be more energised.

- **The industry you're trading in** – certain industries dictate a particular kind of business persona. If you're setting up in the banking and finance sector, your brand is likely to be more formal and restrained than if you're setting up in the gaming, music or media sectors, for example.

- **The types of customers you're targeting** – your target customers will also dictate the nature of your brand. If you're a B2C business aiming at people in the 16-20 age range, your brand, tone and content style will be very different than if you're a B2B business selling to senior buyers in the pharmaceutical industry.

Outline your style and tone

When you're writing content – whether it's a blog on your website, or an email to a customer – the style and tone you use need to reflect your brand.

Consistency is absolutely vital, however small your startup may be at present. As you grow and take on more people in the team, having your brand style clearly defined makes it much easier to keep your content uniform, consistent and 'on brand'.

- **Think about the words you use** – for many startups, sticking to a plain English approach is best. Don't use long words, jargon or abbreviations unless they're absolutely necessary and use the same language you would in person.

- **Keep things simple** – The simpler your language is, the more clearly your content will get your key messages and unique selling points (USPs) across to your audience. So, aim for simplicity in all your written content. There's more on this in Chapter 4, Improving Your Writing.

- **Adopt a tone that mirrors your brand personality** – the brand tone you choose has to be in line with your chosen personality as a business. Keep your tone professional and informative, if that's your brand. Or be friendly, approachable and chatty, if that mirrors the overarching personality of the startup.

Set out some simple guidelines on this tone-of-voice and make sure it's consistent across all your content.

Reflect this brand in your design

Your logo, colours and design go a long way to creating the initial impact of your written content. So put plenty of thought into the visual identity of your startup.

If you can afford it, hire a professional brand designer to do this work for you. They're experts in visual communication and the investment will be worth it – and certainly better than spending hours dabbling in a design app, like Canva, to get a decent result.

Make sure your brand name is unique

If you're trading as a business, you'll no doubt already have a company brand name. But do make sure that the name you've chosen is unique in your market sector – and also that it translates well into other languages if you're eventually aiming for a global reach.

A quick Google search can very quickly show if you've chosen a pre-existing name, or if there's a similar brand name already in existence. This will be important from a search engine optimisation (SEO) perspective once you buy a domain and set up your website.

Similarly, put your intended name into Google Translate, or a similar translation app, and see how your brilliant brand name translates into other key international languages. For example, 'Plopp' is a popular chocolate bar in Sweden, but the name translates less well for an English-speaking audience.

On the whole, your brand name needs to be unique, memorable and easy to search for online. With those boxes ticked, you make it as easy as possible for customers to find you.

Pull everything together into a brand guidelines document

Once you've pinned down your brand and tone, get it all down in writing and create a full set of 'brand guidelines' for your startup.

Include a short summary of your key vision, and summarise your brand personality, writing style and tone, and visual identity. This gives you some solid foundations to work from when writing. It also makes it easier when working with outside contractors, designers or new people that join your startup team as you expand.

KEY TAKEAWAY: Create a brand that reflects who you are as a business

4: Improve Your Writing – Readability and grammar

Right, let's get stuck into the actual writing now… (about time, right!)

We've built up the foundations of your startup vision, customer profiles and brand persona – now we need to polish up your writing skills.

And the main thing to remember here is that we are ALL writers – we write content regularly every day, whether it's emails, texts, Facebook updates or shopping lists. So, don't think of writing as something scary. It isn't!

Forget what you learned at school

Many of the writing methods, grammar rules and traditional language you learned at school don't work well in the context of modern content writing.

You need to get your spelling right, naturally. And it's important to know the right places to put a full stop or a comma. But beyond that, if it sounds right and makes sense, then feel free to go freestyle and mix up your style.

So, for example, despite what your English teacher may have said, you CAN start a sentence with 'And…' and 'But…'. Take a look at any broadsheet newspaper, business website or well-written novel and you'll find examples of starting a sentence with a conjunction (that's a 'joining word').

There are no hard and fast 'rules' of writing, so throw your preconceptions out of the window and just let the words flow. When it comes to writing your content, it's important to not feel constrained by a set of grammar guidelines. This isn't an exam, remember, it's about expressing your enthusiasm and energy for your product.

Start with your key message

In most online and digital content, it's vital to get your important message across quickly. So always start by putting your key message in the opening paragraph.

Tell people what you're going to tell them, get your hook into your reader and give the Google spiders something to search for, with keywords, hashtags and search terms (more on this later).

Keep it simple stupid!

Short, simple, concise content is what works best.

Being long-winded, wordy and using archaic language impresses no-one and definitely won't help your content find an audience.

What's important, is getting your message across clearly. And the best way to do this is usually in the most straightforward terms. That doesn't mean dumbing down or removing personality and individuality from your writing. It means understanding your topic, highlighting the most important elements and explaining them clearly. Makes sense really, doesn't it?

So, the key to good writing is a simple one:

Keep it simple, stupid! (making a handy acronym – KISS).

- Focus on your message and make it clear
- Don't use 50 words when 10 will do the job
- Get your idea across without using jargon
- Throw away anything that doesn't help your message

Aim for maximum readability

We engage with online content best when it's 'chunked up' into small bite-size sections.

This may be a sign of our overuse of social media, but most people are unwilling to commit too much time for reading long, cumbersome and meandering content. Remember, you're not writing War & Peace here. You want to make the words you write as readable as possible and there are a few tricks that will help you do this.

For maximum readability:

- **Keep sentences short** – be concise and don't write long, wandering sentences. Make the full stop your friend and only make each sentence as long as it needs to be. But also mix up sentence lengths. To create variety (like this).

- **Use plenty of breaks** – break up long paragraphs with spaces, so the text doesn't look so daunting to the reader and has room to breathe. And pull out key messages and sentences so they stand out from the main body text.

- **Include sub-headings to create clear sections** – use a subheading to introduce a new idea or a new theme in the content. This helps readers to scan down the margin and see what your blog/email/article is about.

- **Use bullet points wisely** – if you're creating a list of ideas or giving a detailed explanation of how to do something, use bullet points to introduce each new item or point (like I've done here).

Contractions and slang are fine

If you're aiming for a more informal, chatty brand persona, it's fine to use some colloquial slang and to shorten words into contractions (things like 'don't' instead of 'do not' and 'you're' instead of 'you are').

Using contractions and everyday slang makes your content easier to read and helps you to connect more directly with your audience.

If you're aiming to create an open and friendly brand persona, sounding human and approachable is key to this – and writing as you speak is an effective way to create more humanity in your content.

Put yourself in your customers' shoes

To write content that your reader finds interesting, you need to think like your customer. Think about their challenges, their pain points or their specific needs as consumers/customers – and write from their perspective.

Writing in the second person helps: e.g. 'When you're looking for the best CRM system for your business…' rather than 'When business owners are looking for the best CRM system for their business'. Make this about MY needs, not YOUR company's offerings.

By directing your content directly at me (the reader and your potential customer), it shows that you understand my customer needs. And this is great for increasing confidence in your brand, positioning your product/services in the busy marketplace and turning your customers into long-term advocates for your brand and company.

Let the music in your writing sing through

Good content writing is about balancing clear, simple language with the descriptive or technical language needed to sell your business vision to customers.

If you can get that balance right, you'll hear those words sing. Don't get too bogged down in the technicalities of grammar – just write as you speak. Be natural and the words will flow.

Keep the KISS acronym in mind when you first sit down to write some content. Read it through and ask yourself 'Am I really making this as simple and effective as I can?'. If not, then it may be time to keep it simple, stupid!

KEY TAKEAWAY: Ignore the rules. Keep it simple and just get writing!

5: Build A Website – Content and messaging

In the digital age, your website is one of the most important assets you have as a business – so it's absolutely vital to put the right thought and planning into your site.

A website is your shop front, your marketing tool, your content hub and the place customers go to when they want to know more about your brand. If you get the content, style, look or user interface wrong, users just won't engage with you – and that means you're essentially turning away potential paying customers!

So how do you go about creating the ideal website?

Here are five key steps that will help you build a site that's effective, easy to use and creates the best level of engagement with your target audience.

Step 1: Focus on your target audience and ideal customer

In Chapter 2, we talked about knowing your ideal customer. Here's where that knowledge comes into play. Keep that audience in mind when you're writing and designing your website.

To keep the site focused:

- **Target your ideal viewer and potential client?** – whether you're a new startup, or an established small business, you've got to know your customers. Understand their needs and find out what they look for in your product. Then you're ready to tailor your website content to meet these needs.

- **Tailor your products, services and content to fit your customer base** – how you present your core products/services, blogs and marketing has to reflect this ideal customer type. Customise your site so it feels like it was designed specifically for them – and make them feel at home.

Step 2: Write your key page content and consider your value

When customers visit your site, they want to quickly know why you're the right product/service for them. So, make it clear. Demonstrate exactly where you add value for your chosen audience, so they don't have to go digging.

Do your homework. Research your target audience. And make sure your site content tells me IMMEDIATELY what you do (and why I'm going to love it).

To begin the web content process:

- **Draft your content as rough key points** – good web content makes the maximum impact with the minimum number of words. Drafting out ideas in a Word or Google doc will give you a basic idea of your messaging and helps you flesh out your wording, pages and site structure.

- **Get a web developer involved from the start** – the sooner you get an experienced web developer involved, the easier building the site will be. Web devs know what works (and what doesn't) and can help you tailor your rough content into workable wireframes (the blueprints from which the site will be built).

- **Make it clear what you do** – website viewers have limited time to find what they're looking for on your site. So, stick to the point, quickly explain your core proposition, and make sure your call-to-action (usually your contact page) is front and centre – so prospects (potential customers) can email or pick up the phone.

- **Talk about the business** – your website isn't just for selling. Your site is also a content hub where you should be sharing blog posts, news updates and business news. It's an important point of contact, so keep it interesting!

Step 3: Make your design and messaging really simple

Working with professional content writers and website designers will speed up the build process. But it's perfectly possible to write your own content, if you put some thought into the process – and follow a few simple rules.

To make your site content a success:

- **Keep it simple!** – if you can describe your product feature in 25 words, don't use 250 words. The more concise and succinct your web copy is, the quicker your viewers will find the information they're looking for.

- **Be clear about what you do** – on your homepage, tell people why they should choose your company. And what it is you do. For example; 'Marketing support for busy startups – making it easy to promote your new product'.

- **Make your site responsive and mobile friendly** – increasingly, people will be viewing your website from their phone screen, not a laptop or desktop machine. So, your website needs to be 'responsive' – in other words, it must automatically resize and reformat when viewed on a mobile device.

- **Bring your branding into the design** – you've already designed your logo, brand colour palette and tone of voice. So, make sure these elements are reflected in your website content and design. It keeps your brand identity consistent and helps customers to recognise your name and logo.

Step 4: Give customers the best user experience

For your website to do its job, it should be easy to use. That means having an effective user interface (UI) – the elements of the site design that viewers interact with to use the site and move around.

It also means offering the best possible user experience (UX), so there are no hurdles, confusing menus or slow downloads of images that stop customers finding what they want. A bad UI, coupled with a poor UX, is not going to convert many prospects!

From the moment viewers land on your site, you want to push them to your chosen end point – whether that's your contact page, team page or the latest product page.

To make the site work like a dream:

- **Have a simple menu** – limit the number of areas in your top menu. Having 5 or 6 key menu items keeps the site straightforward and makes it easy to navigate. Having more pages is good for search engine optimisation (SEO), but a simple menu architecture helps the viewer find your key content.

- **Put your key message 'above the fold'** – make sure customers can see your main proposition at the top of the page, without scrolling down. On a mobile, that's the first thing they'll see, so keep them engaged (and less likely to 'bounce' off the page).

- **Be strategic with calls-to-action** – think carefully about the positioning of buttons and calls-to-action. If you want viewers to contact you, put the 'Contact us' button at both the top and bottom of the page (you can't be sure people will scroll to the end).

Step 5: Measure performance, customer feedback and ROI

A website is an evolving and changing beast. So once your site is live, continue to update it, post fresh content and review how well your pages are performing. This helps to refine the effectiveness of your content and keep your SEO performing well.

- **Use analytics to measure site performance** – track the performance and return-on-investment (ROI) of your online content and update your content planning accordingly. There's more on this in Chapter 10, Analyse Performance.

- **Display customer feedback and authority ratings** – demonstrate your trustworthiness through backlinks to outside sources, such as independent customer ratings sites (TrustPilot for example) or by including great testimonial quotes from your satisfied customers.

Keep evolving: your website is never finished

For a startup that wants to raise its brand profile, a website is such a valuable asset. So it's important to nurture your site and look for new ways to improve it. Pressing 'publish' isn't the end of the website creation process – in fact, it's just the beginning.

To make your site work hard, measure your online performance, post frequent new content and evolve to meet any new online challenges and opportunities.

Remember:

- Focus your website directly at your target customers
- Write your content first – so you get your key messaging sorted early
- Make your design and messaging simple – with your proposition up front
- Deliver the best user experience – and give your customers what they want.
- Keep posting and updating content

KEY TAKEAWAY: Build a website that quickly (and simply) explains who you are

6: Have A Content Plan – Planning and timelines

Your website is up and running (hurray!). And now you're eager to start writing and firing out blogs left, right and centre. But, as with all things in business, your content will be far more effective if you put some thought and planning behind your content pipeline.

The more targeted, organised and planned out your content is, the more likely it will be to achieve your goals. So, there's considerable value in putting some time aside to create a proper content plan for your startup.

Write a content plan for the year

Having a yearly content plan puts some real impetus behind your content creation, but it needn't be a hugely complex thing to set up. You can dive into detailed planning if you want to, but to start off with it's a good idea to start simple – don't turn this into an unwieldy task to add to your growing to-do list.

To create a high-level plan for the year:

- **Go simple with a spreadsheet** – the easiest way to start a content plan is to use an Excel or GSheet spreadsheet. Break your spreadsheet down with months or weeks along one axis, and content ideas on the other axis. Quickly capture your ideas for blogs and campaigns across the period and give yourself a rough outline and timescale to measure yourself against.

- **Get interactive with online tools** – there are plenty of online 'to-do list' style apps that can be useful to use. Tools like Trello or ToDoist are a step up from a spreadsheet but keep things simple enough for the novice to stay productive. Create lists and cards, full of your content ideas, and use the deadline and notification tools to remind you when content is due to be written and published.

- **Go deep with project management apps** – if you want to get really granular with your planning and workstreams, there's a big choice of cloud-based marketing planning tools on the market. Apps like Asana and HubSpot will keep you organised and productive, with all the software bells and whistles you need.

Identify key themes and topics that you need to tackle

With a template, spreadsheet or online planning list ready to be populated, the next step is to start considering the key topics and messaging you want to include.

Have a think about the main topics you want to cover with your content, and the ideal client personas you're aiming this content at. Rough out some blog titles, campaign ideas and social media content based on these themes/personas to start fleshing out some of these topic areas. And remember to keep your content varied, frequent and focused – so these topics will give you the return on investment you're after.

Outline your monthly content needs

With a bit more clarity around your topics, it's a good idea to think about what channels you're planning on using, and how frequently you want to be posting.

The amount of content you produce, and the frequency of your content creation, will be driven by the time and marketing resources you have available. If you're the founder and busy getting the startup off the ground, you're not going to have much time to write long-form blog posts. But if you've got a team you can delegate to (or have chosen to outsource the writing to a professional) then you can increase your content aspirations.

Set some clear targets for content frequency:

- Will you write one blog per month, and a customer newsletter every quarter that summarises your key messages?

- Or do you want to write a blog per week and run an email campaign per month to re-purpose and promote this content?

- And think about your social media frequency too. Will you be posting daily and reacting to customer and supplier messages?

Set timescales, milestones and deadlines

Nothing motivates like a looming deadline (although you may need a few shots of coffee to get those writing brain cells firing). So, having clear timescales and deadlines for each piece of content will help you stay organised.

Once you've outlined a content idea – whether it's a blog, an email or a Twitter post – set a deadline for drafting, reviewing and posting this piece of content. Where possible, tie these timescales in with your overall business planning, so you've got content ready to support a new product launch, or to highlight a discount event.

Put these dates in your online diary, or set them as deadlines in your planning app, so you'll have a visual overview of when things are due – and will get some polite nudges and notifications from your software to keep you productive.

KEY TAKEAWAY: Create an annual content plan to stay organised and productive

7: Get Blogging – Telling stories

Blogging is an area of content writing that everyone will tell you is essential – but writing a blog is not something that comes naturally to everyone.

Blog posts provide your startup with a regular way to share useful, topical or valuable content with your customers – whether it's talking about a customer issue, covering your viewpoint on a topical news story, or outlining how a new product feature adds value.

But, at base level, blogging is about telling a story and building a narrative around your key theme, topic or messaging. As such, you need to learn to be a good storyteller. And that's going to require inspiration, creativity and a way with words.

Have a regular pipeline of topics

Inspiration is an elusive beast. Some days you'll be overflowing with exciting topics to blog about. Other days your mind will be utterly devoid of good ideas. So, when you ARE feeling inspired, or a new idea pops into your head, get it written down fast!

Add blog ideas to your content plan as you think of them, and make sure there's a regular flow of content for you to work from. Where possible, have the next month's blog ideas planned out a month in advance (at the very least), so you keep the flow and pace of your content and don't have any nasty gaps when inspiration is low.

Don't make blogs a sales tool

A blog post isn't a direct sales tool. It's not a landing page for your new product, or a piece of marketing collateral to promote your latest sale. In short, a blog is not for ramming your sales agenda down someone's throat.

A blog post is a good story, or a shared opinion, or a helpful piece of advice. Your blog posts exist to share useful content and, by doing so, position you, your people and your brand as trusted experts in your industry or marketplace.

Get your blogs the right length

A common question from newbie bloggers is 'How long should my blog post be?'. There's no right answer to this, but it is important to think about the word count, the amount of text on the page and how likely people are to read the whole shebang.

Some people love short blog posts they can read in two minutes. Other people love in-depth, long-form blogs that might take 10 or 15 minutes to read. Find out what your customers prefer and track your engagement levels to see which blogs are working best (and use this to inform your content strategy).

Here's a rough guide to blog length to get you started:

- **Short blog posts (300-500 words)** – if you want to say something short and sweet, and have a single clear message to communicate, keep the post short. 300 words is the absolute minimum (Google won't rank the page otherwise). Any more than 500 words and you'll start to lose focus on your single key message.

- **Medium-length blog posts (750-1,000 words)** – When your topic's a meaty one, and there are several key messages to include, you'll need a bigger word count. This gives readers more depth and detail but isn't so long that it can't be read in one sitting. The average adult reads about 300 words per minute, so a 900-word blog post will take most people around 3 minutes to read.

- **Long-form blog posts (1,500-2,500+ words)** –
  Longer posts do get good SEO results and offer
  more value to customers and prospects who are
  interested in your main topic. Aiming for a 2,000-
  word post will take more writing time, and people
  will expect you to have done your research. On the
  whole, the key to a good long-form post is to avoid
  waffle, break up the body text into plenty of sections
  and to choose a topic that will interest your key
  audience.

Tell interesting stories

People love to read real stories, whether that's a customer
case study, a post about someone in the team, or coverage
of your latest customer event.

Writing about real events and real people takes your blog
content out of the formal structure of 'business content'
and creates a more honest and engaging narrative. Your
writing can become more expressive, you can emphasise
the emotional impact and it's possible to create content
that really pushes the human angle of your brand.

To humanise your content:

- **Learn to tell a story** – Introduce me to the person, team or business that you're profiling and explain what they're about. Explain what challenge they had, what their goal was or why they needed your products/services. And tell me how the story ended – did they overcome the challenge? Did they achieve their goal? Did the tale end well?

- **Engage your reader** – make a key point and engage people in the concepts you're aiming to get across. If your topic relates to a core challenge that your audience is facing, they're all the more likely to read your content.

- **Keep it real, human and non-sales** – Stories are about humans, not products. Even if you're a product manufacturer, talk about how PEOPLE are using your product, how it's made their lives easier, or how your business has evolved to meet the human needs of your customers. In other words, how have you changed their lives?

Have a voice: apply your style and tone

Your blog content needs to be consistent with the other content you produce as a business. Make sure that the words/language you use, and the tone you adopt, fit with your brand guidelines and give your blogs a uniform persona, while still getting across the individual personalities and ideas of your various team members.

Make your blogs easy to read

Aim for maximum readability, so don't write 2,000 words of plain text with no spacing that will look daunting and unwelcoming to your readers.

Break content up into short paragraphs, use sub-headings to section up your key points and use bullet points to create helpful lists of the important ideas. The more you work on the readability of your content, the more these tricks will become second nature.

10 ways to improve your business blogging

The more blogging you do, the better your posts will become. As with any kind of writing, it's about putting in the hours, getting used to the format and learning what works well (and what falls flat on its behind).

To help you speed up the learning process, here are 10 key ways for quickly improving your business blogging:

1. **Blogs are not landing pages** – don't write a blog post as if you were writing a landing page for your new product. Think about opinions, stories and avoiding the hard sell.

2. **Blog about something you have a passion for** – if you're going to write a post, the theme really HAS to be something you have some genuine interest in.

3. **Be honest and genuine** – for customers to engage with your blog posts, they'll want to feel that they're getting 'the real you' from the words you write.

4. **Steer clear of technical jargon** – every industry has jargon but remember that many customers won't understand these technical terms and abbreviations.

5. **Give readers something useful** – if people are going to invest their precious time in reading your content, you need to give them something valuable.

6. **Post content as frequently as possible** – a blog has to be kept updated, or your followers will just lose interest and won't interact with your content.

7. **Comment on topical themes** – a good blog is topical, current and at the cutting edge of what's going on in your industry, market or sector.

8. **Think about keywords and SEO** – titles, opening paragraphs and body text MUST include relevant keywords, to increase search engine optimisation (SEO).

9. **Use images in your blogs and social media promotion** – images, photos and graphics all catch the eye and add to your blog's engagement levels.

10. **Consider vlogging or podcasts** – If you're more of a 'talker' than a 'writer', video and podcasts can be quick ways to share your ideas with the world.

KEY TAKEAWAY: Tell good stories, add value and avoid the hard sell

8: Start Getting Social – Tweeting and sharing

Your website and blog are two key channels when it comes to publishing and sharing your startup's content. But to get your message out there effectively, a social media presence has become a necessity for any forward-thinking startup.

Social media channels are increasingly vital for your marketing; both to interact with your customers, and to promote and share your existing website content.

So, which social media platforms should you use? And how do you tailor and repurpose your content to maximise your impact through social?

Choose the same social channels your customers use

Building a loyal social media following will help your social accounts to become invaluable tools in your digital marketing armoury.

It's important that the social media platforms you opt to use as a business reflect those used by your target audience. There's no point being all over Instagram if your core customer demographic are all Facebook people.

To get started with social media:

- **Do your research** – look into the various social media providers and see which platforms your competitors use, which are the most popular for your industry and where the people in your existing network are posting and interacting.

- **Think about customer personas** – go back to your customer personas (see Chapter 2, Know Your Audience) and research which platforms resonate most closely with your ideal customer personas. Ultimately, you want your social content to appear in the places frequented by your target audience.

- **Choose the most relevant platforms** – the social platforms you use have to align with the type of business you are. For example, if you're a law firm, there's little point in focusing on SnapChat, as your core 35-55 age range professional audience are unlikely to be using this particular platform.

Start with the Holy Social Trinity

As a starting point, Twitter, LinkedIn and Facebook are the three platforms that will make up your core 'Holy Social Trinity' – helping you cover the main social bases.

- **Twitter is all about micro-blogging**, posting snappy online messages called 'tweets' to your followers. With a 280-character limit on each post, Twitter keeps things succinct, whilst also allowing you to attach photos, graphics or videos with each tweet. It's a fast-paced, informal platform that's well suited for both B2B and B2C companies.

- **LinkedIn is about professional networking**, helping your brand to connect with other brands and professionals in your sector. Content is usually longer and more in-depth than on Twitter, with no upper limit on characters or words in a post. It's a more formal and corporate platform and probably most suited to B2B companies.

- **Facebook is the most 'social' of the three core platforms**, with the focus on sharing your brand's daily life with customers and followers. It's good for photos, videos and reaching a wide consumer audience, but can be of limited value to professional B2B companies – unless you're looking to raise community engagement.

Other social platforms to consider

Aside from Twitter, LinkedIn and Facebook, there's a wide range of other social media, photo-sharing and video content platforms that may be suited to your startup.

Some popular platforms include:

- **YouTube** – if you're creating video marketing, vlogs, video case studies or recorded webinars, YouTube will be an essential channel to use – it's where your video content will live and where your followers can interact with this content.

- **Instagram** – profiling your startup through innovative photography and images gives another edge to your marketing. Instagram gives you a very visual way to market the business directly to your followers.

- **Flickr** – Flickr is another photo-sharing platform, but with a focus on higher-resolution, well-shot quality images (rather than the filters and hashtags you're more likely to see on Instagram).

- **SnapChat** – If you're looking to target a younger audience, Snapchat is worth considering as a channel. Principally, it's a chat app, but there are also innovative ways to share video, stories and content with your followers.

- **Medium** – not a social platform, per se, Medium is a great place for sharing long-form articles and opinion pieces, helping you to position yourself as a thought leader or go-to adviser in your particular startup niche or industry specialism.

Keep your social content snappy

Generally speaking, your main social media accounts are not the place for long, meandering posts. Keep your social posts and updates short, snappy and to the point.

Our attention spans in the digital 21st century are short. Readers will ignore or discount your updates if they take more than a few seconds to grasp your message. This is especially true of Twitter where you only have 280 characters to play with. If you can say what you need to in 5 words, don't use 50. Aim for brevity at all times.

Use hashtags wisely

Hashtags (#killercontent – like this) are the tags that allow people to search for and find specific topics and themes within your social content.

By adding a # in front of a word or phrase (with no spaces or punctuation) you create a searchable term within your social content. Adding relevant hashtags helps with engagement and SEO, allowing you to interact with the right audiences.

Think about what your potential customers would type into Google when searching and write your hashtags around the right keywords and search terms.

Think visually

Words are important. But the human eye is more easily attracted by visual images. So, make sure you think carefully about using images and graphics in your social content.

Adding photos, images, graphics and infographics to social posts improves your engagement levels. Try pairing an image with the content you write and see the uplift in views and likes. Video is also effective in raising engagement, although you'll need to keep any social videos under the 2-3 minutes, ideally.

Post social content regularly!

Social media platforms and their users love frequent posts and content. Posting regularly is good for both your SEO and for keeping your engagement levels high with followers, prospects and existing customers.

There's obviously a time commitment to planning, writing, finalising and publishing content. But you can use tools like Hootsuite to automatically schedule your pre-written content and keep that pipeline of posts coming.
Have fun with your social

Ultimately, you want your social content to attract followers, deliver higher levels of engagement and enhance your overall brand profile in the market. But don't forget to have fun with your social content along the way.

Injecting some humour, energy and innovation into your posts and content is a good way to make your social posts stand out. Take a look at the Museum of English Rural Life's Twitter account @TheMERL to see how a quirky, humorous social personality can help to liven up your online presence and bring in more followers.

KEY TAKEAWAY: Post regularly, interact with customers and build a following.

9: Run A Campaign – Email, newsletters and ads

Your website is up and running, and you're posting regular content via your blog and social channels. Now's the time to ramp up your digital marketing and start thinking about targeted campaigns to promote your products/services.

What's a campaign?

A marketing campaign is a planned series of content aimed at promoting a specific product, service or customer offer. With so many different digital marketing channels now available to us, a key part of planning and running a campaign is using the right digital and social channels to promote your key messages.

You might run an email campaign that links back to a new product landing page on your website. Or you might post a series of Twitter posts that link to a new blog post. The key is to have a central aim for the campaign, a clear call-to-action (what you want readers to do) and a carefully organised plan and timescale for your campaign.

Email campaigns and direct email marketing

Email may be 'old tech' but it's still used by many of us on a daily basis. As such, a well-planned email campaign can be an effective way to get your brand and/or products in front of the right target audience.

Important areas to consider when planning an email campaign will include:

- **Make the campaign targeted** – don't use a 'throw enough mud at the wall and see what sticks' approach to targeting your email campaign. The key is to profile a very specific customer segment with a highly targeted campaign, allowing you to position your messaging and get good results/engagement.

- **Keep your copy short** – a long, wordy email will be ignored. People simply don't have time to read 500 words about your exciting new product. Keep your content as short as possible (150-300 words, ideally) and use subheadings and bullet points to break up the body text and maintain the readability (think back to the KISS mantra in Chapter 4).

- **Have one, clear call-to-action** – if you include multiple links, buttons and calls-to-action, your end reader will get confused. Stick to one very obvious call-to-action (a registration page, a landing page or a contact page etc.) and make it easy for your potential customers to navigate the email.

NOTE: Data protection law and GDPR regulations mean you MUST have approval from any prospects/customers before you can email them with marketing. So, make sure you have the right approvals before sending out any campaign. You also need to include an 'Unsubscribe' button for those people that want to opt out.

Email newsletters

Rounding up your published content into a regular newsletter definitely isn't a new idea. But it's a quick and effective way to wrap up previous content into a format that existing customers will find appealing, increasing the reach of your message... if you get it right.

Whether you opt for a hard-copy mailshot (not advised from a sustainability perspective), an email newsletter or links to news pieces on your website, the same overall approach applies.

- **Include interesting content** – as the founder, you obviously think EVERYTHING about your new business is fascinating. But take care to include content that's of real-world interest to your target customer audience. Keep it relevant, offer practical tips and include engaging content like staff profiles, news updates or customer competitions etc.

- **Don't waffle** – keep the introduction to your newsletter short and personable, and quickly list the main blog posts/news stories/feature updates that you want to highlight. The more concise you can be, the better – as a reader, I should be able to scan through this email and quickly pick out the bits I want to engage with.

- **Link to the full content** – for digital comms, it's most effective to include a short, pithy summary and then include a link to the full article/story. If you're lucky, readers will click through, getting more traffic to your site and giving a new lease of life to pre-published and older content.

- **Keep things regular** – I keep banging on about regular content, but it's a vital consideration for a newsletter. If you're going to start producing a customer newsletter, you need to publish it on time, at the same point in the month/year every time. It's this regularity that helps you build up a good readership.

Campaign landing pages

Having a landing page for your campaign gives you a home for the relevant content and helps you drive traffic back to your website. With a specific campaign page, you can also easily track and measure engagement levels for the campaign (there's more on analytics in Chapter 10).

Your campaign landing page is part of the company's website. It can be public and included in your main menus, or it can be hidden and only accessible from the link you use in your emails, social posts and other campaign marketing.

To get the best from a campaign landing page:

- **Have an effective strapline and intro** – having a strapline for your campaign means writing a short, memorable sentence that will stick in customer's minds. A concise one or two-line teaser also helps to introduce what your campaign is about.

- **Think about design** – the layout and design of the landing page is important. Your strapline and intro need to be eye-catching and appealing to a potential customer, so put some real thought into the aesthetics of the page. Where possible, work with a good web designer to maximise the design elements.

- **Keeping the content focused** – the messaging on the page must be highly targeted towards your intended audience. This isn't a broad-stroke product page; you're aiming to get one very specific message across to (generally) one very specific target audience – so stick to the point and don't meander.

- **Make your call-to-action obvious** – if you want people to click a 'Buy now' button, or fill out a contact form, make that as clear and unambiguous as possible. Keep the layout clean and uncluttered and put your call-to-action front and centre of the page design.

Paid ads and PPC etc.

Digital advertising allows you to get incredibly granular with your targeting, with sites like Facebook offering in-depth profiling of targets and Google offering plenty of tools to get your digital ads in front of the right eyes.

Using paid advertising or pay-per-click (PPC) helps to increase the chances of potential customers seeing your banner ads and digital marketing. Rather than relying on organic searches and SEO, paid advertising helps you target a specific customer group or demographic. With PPC, you then pay a small fee every time a user clicks through from your advert.

If increasing your enquiries, sales and revenues is a key aim for the startup, paid advertising can be a good way to give your business development and sales a boost, but there is a cost associated with this approach.

When using paid advertising:

- **Get detailed with targeting** – as with all digital marketing, the path to success is being extremely targeted with your paid advertising. Think about the age, location, income bracket or buying habits of your ideal campaign customer and use these elements to target potential customers at the most micro level.

- **Keep your messaging tight** – small banners have very limited real estate for content and graphics. Google ads, for example, allow only 90 characters of text, so you will need to be VERY concise with your use of content. A short title and one short heading are really all you have to play with.

- **Use clear buttons and links** – If your banner ad includes a specific call-to-action, such as 'Buy now', make sure the button or link is easily seen, obvious and links through to the right campaign landing page or contact page.

- **Track engagement and retarget** – once a potential customer has engaged with your site, this data can be used to 'retarget' them with additional ads. If a prospect has clicked through to a specific product page, you can then retarget them with ads for similar products, or when there's a discount on the product etc.

Creating and managing a campaign plan

Keeping on top of a campaign can get complicated, especially if you're new to digital marketing and the intricacies of the different digital channels.

To stay in control of your marketing campaign, you need a campaign plan – in the same way that you needed a content plan for your content in Chapter 6. Your campaign plan works in the same way, but with a smaller timeframe and a more targeted focus on the main theme behind your chosen campaign.

- **Decide which channels to use** – you don't need to use all available digital channels for every campaign. Use the digital marketing and social media channels that best suit the job for your chosen theme and audience.

- **Plan out the activity** – use your project management tool of choice to plan out the campaign activity, day-by-day or week-by-week, with clear deadlines for each channel and associated task.

- **Manage your progress** – keep track of progress and mark off each task as it's completed. By sticking to the planned deadlines, running campaigns needn't be an overwhelming or stressful task. Just take each item one at a time.

- **Use software tools to help** – project management tools like Asana and Trello make the whole process of planning and remembering each piece of activity much easier. They can also be set up to send notifications and reminders.

KEY TAKEAWAY: Target your audience, use the right channels and plan activity

10: Analyse Performance – Engagement and analytics

You've written lots of exciting blogs and content, you've fired it out into the world and now you can sit back and relax, right? Wrong!

Publishing the content isn't the end story, you also need to track and measure the performance of this content, and see which posts get an audience (and which posts fall into a content black hole, never to be seen again).

The power of digital data

One of the key benefits of digital marketing in the 21st century is that the whole process is driven by data – data that's tracked and recorded over the course of your campaigns. This data is a mine of useful information, giving you empirical evidence of which blog posts are most popular, which product pages are getting most traffic, or which paid ads are giving you the best return on your marketing budget etc.

I'm no 'data warrior' – I'm a writer by trade, after all. But you'd be foolish to ignore the potential power of tracking, analysing and reacting to the data that your content marketing and social activity is generating for the business.

Getting the most from your analytics

The stats, graphs, jargon and lists of numbers in an analytics report can look a bit daunting at first – especially if, like me, you're not a numbers person. But with a very small amount of reading up and education, you can start using your analytics to add some real value to your content creation process.

To start using your analytics more effectively:

- **Do the Google Analytics training** – Google Academy offers free training on analytics and how to measure the acquisition, behaviour and conversion rates of your content. If you're completely new to website and marketing analytics, this is a great way to get started and learn the basics.

- **Regularly review your stats** – Google Analytics links to your website, and the main social media platforms also include their own statistics and analytics tools to track acquisition and conversion etc. Look at your stats on a regular basis to see which blogs are getting read, which Twitter posts got retweeted and which campaign landing pages received the most love.

- **Inform your content strategy** – look at the results from your analytics to pin down the content that really delivers, and review your approach, your tactics and your content ideas in your content plan – so you're constantly updating, refining and improving your content approach.

Content doesn't stand still

Your content marketing isn't a static process that's written in stone. The digital channels that work well now may see a slump in engagement as new platforms become available, and the content themes that get great engagement may alter and evolve over the business life of your new startup. The key is to react to this.

In the same way that your startup will react to changing market forces and evolving customer needs, your content needs to also have this ability to flex and react.

Keep an eye on your analytics, keep abreast of new developments in digital marketing, and talk to customers to see what topics and themes they're actually interested in. By continually revising and modernising your content strategy, you'll keep your website, blog and digital campaigns fresh and vibrant.

KEY TAKEAWAY: Use analytics to inform and improve your use of content

Conclusion: Keep writing! – putting it all into practice

Having breezed your way through all ten chapters of this book, you're now prepped and ready to start writing killer content for your startup!

As with all new challenges in a startup, getting the best from your content marketing is going to take time. There will be hiccups, challenges and failures along the way – but that's all part of the experience of running your own business. The key is to knuckle down and get on with it – start writing, start creating and start getting your messages out there to prospects, customers and other people in your market.

Just follow these ten steps to killer content:

1. Define Your Vision – Have a core vision and know WHY you're in business

A startup with a core vision behind it is the best possible starting point for any content marketing. Define the 'why' of why you're in business and put this front and centre of your brand, your messaging and your digital marketing and social content.

2. Know Your Audience – Know your customers, and target them effectively

To target your audience effectively, you need a crystal-clear definition of your ideal customer. Create a fully formed outline of this perfect customer, and tailor your digital marketing and targeted advertising to capture this specific audience.

3. Create Your Brand – Create a brand that reflects who you are as a business

Your brand reflects who you are in the market. So, create a personality, tone and style that tells your regular customers what you stand for, and that attracts new enquiries and prospects to the brand identity you're reflecting in your digital marketing.

4. Improve Your Writing – Ignore the rules. Keep it simple and just get writing!

Do your best to get the grammar and spelling right. But, ultimately, don't feel constrained by the rules. Write from the heart, write with passion and improve the readability of your content through hard work and practice.

5. Build A Website – Build a website that quickly explains who you are

Your company website is a shop window for your products and/or services. But it's also the central hub for all your digital marketing activity. Make sure the site tells people what you do, what you care about and how you're going to add value for customers.

6. Have A Content Plan – Create an annual content plan to stay organised

Content works better when there's a plan driving it. Create an annual plan for your content and marketing activity and make this the route map for your content creation over the year – and remember to update the plan as circumstances evolve.

7. Get Blogging – Tell good stories, add value and avoid the hard sell

A blog is a great channel for engaging with your prospects and customers. Find the topics you're passionate about and share your thoughts, opinions and practical advice with your audience – and position yourselves as experts in your niche.

8. Start Getting Social – Post regularly and interact with your customers

Social media accounts give you direct, two-way communication with prospects and customers. Choose the most effective social platforms and use your social content to interact with followers and support and enhance your digital marketing.

9. Run A Campaign – Target an audience, use the right channels and plan activity

A campaign brings together all the big guns to help you promote one specific message. Use a selection of your digital and social channels, from landing pages, emails, blogs and social content, to target a specific audience with your core call-to-action.

10. Analyse Performance – Use analytics to inform and improve your content

Analytics track and record the performance of your website and content marketing. Use this goldmine of data to refine your marketing strategy, improve your content approach and gradually evolve and enhance the effectiveness of your marketing return.

Put the theory into practice – and keep improving

The quality of your writing, and the value of your content marketing, will only get better through repeated practice. The more content you create, the better you'll get at nailing the perfect blog, or the most engaging campaign landing page.

By applying the ten steps, you'll have a defined vision, brand and content strategy – and the chops to produce content that will truly engage with your ideal customers.

Keep writing, keep flexing and see the difference that a well-thought-through content strategy can have on the future success of your startup!

About the author

Steve is an experienced content writer, having worked in marketing for PwC, as a content writer in Xero's marketing team and content manager for The Profitable Firm.

He now runs his own CommsBreakdown content writing business, providing bespoke content, branding and digital marketing concepts to a cross section of tech startups, fintech companies, established businesses and accounting firms.

Steve lives in Hertfordshire with his partner, Joanna, and their young daughter. When he's not writing, he'll be found playing guitar, making bad techno and attempting to ration his coffee and chocolate intake.

Contact Steve on Twitter @CommsBreakdown

Printed in Poland
by Amazon Fulfillment
Poland Sp. z o.o., Wrocław